The Machine

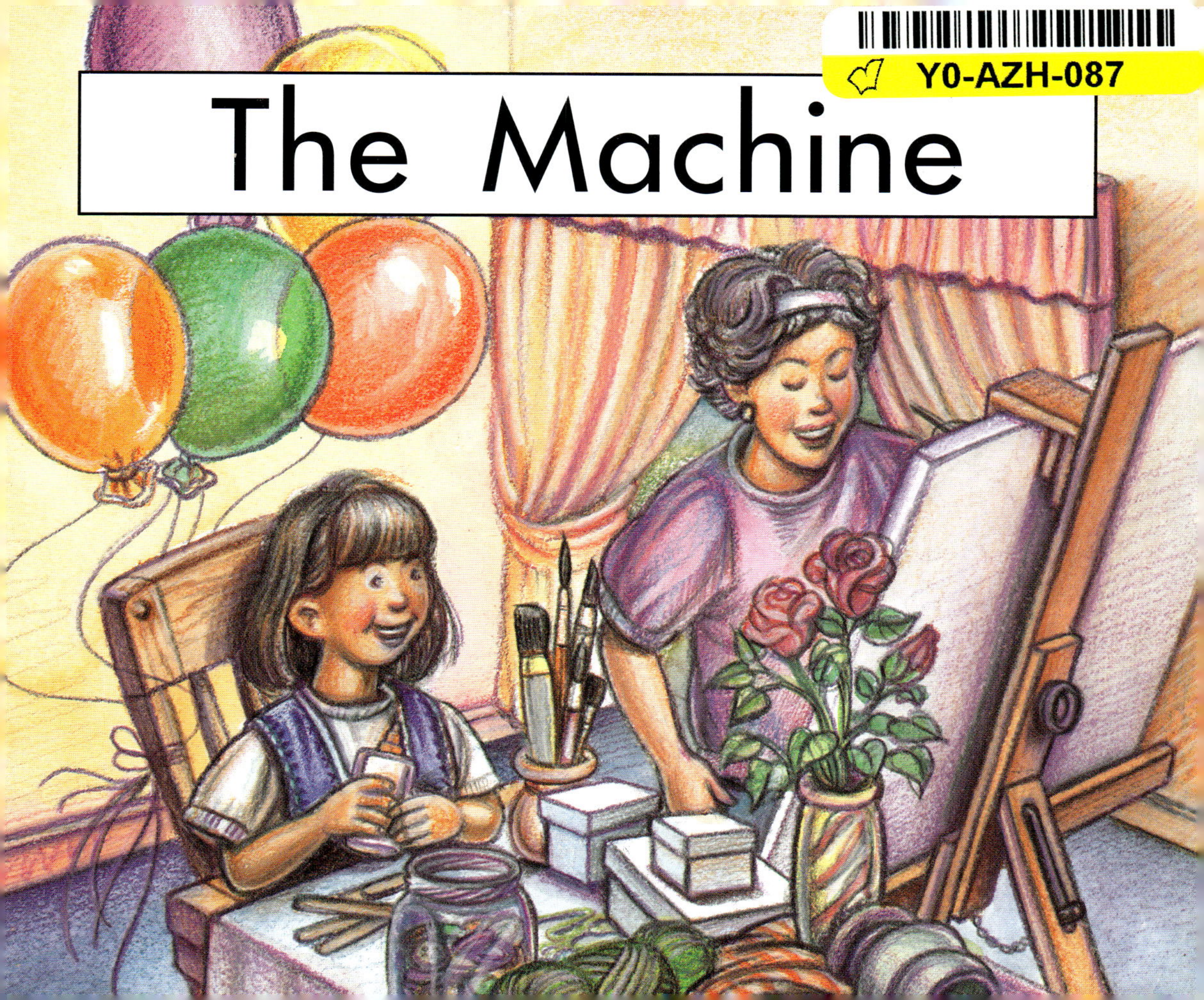

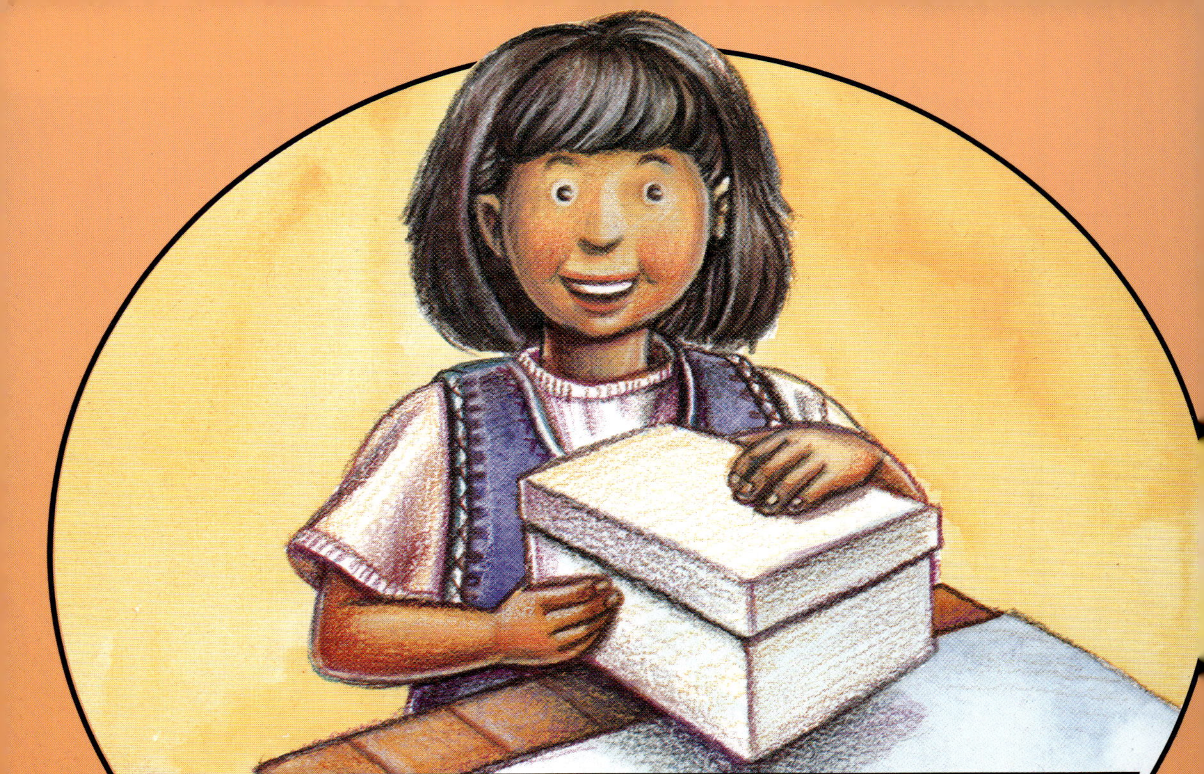

I have one big box.

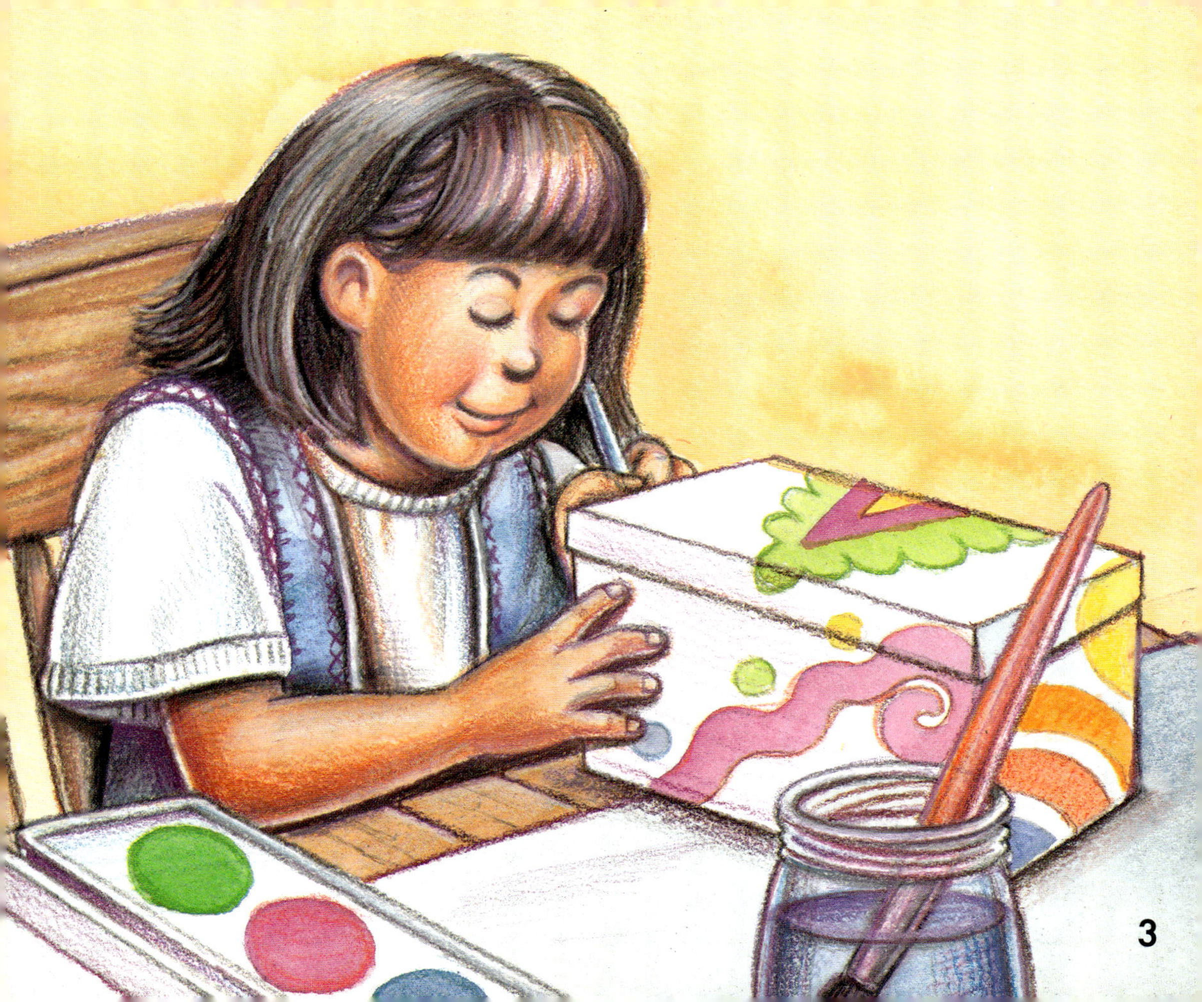

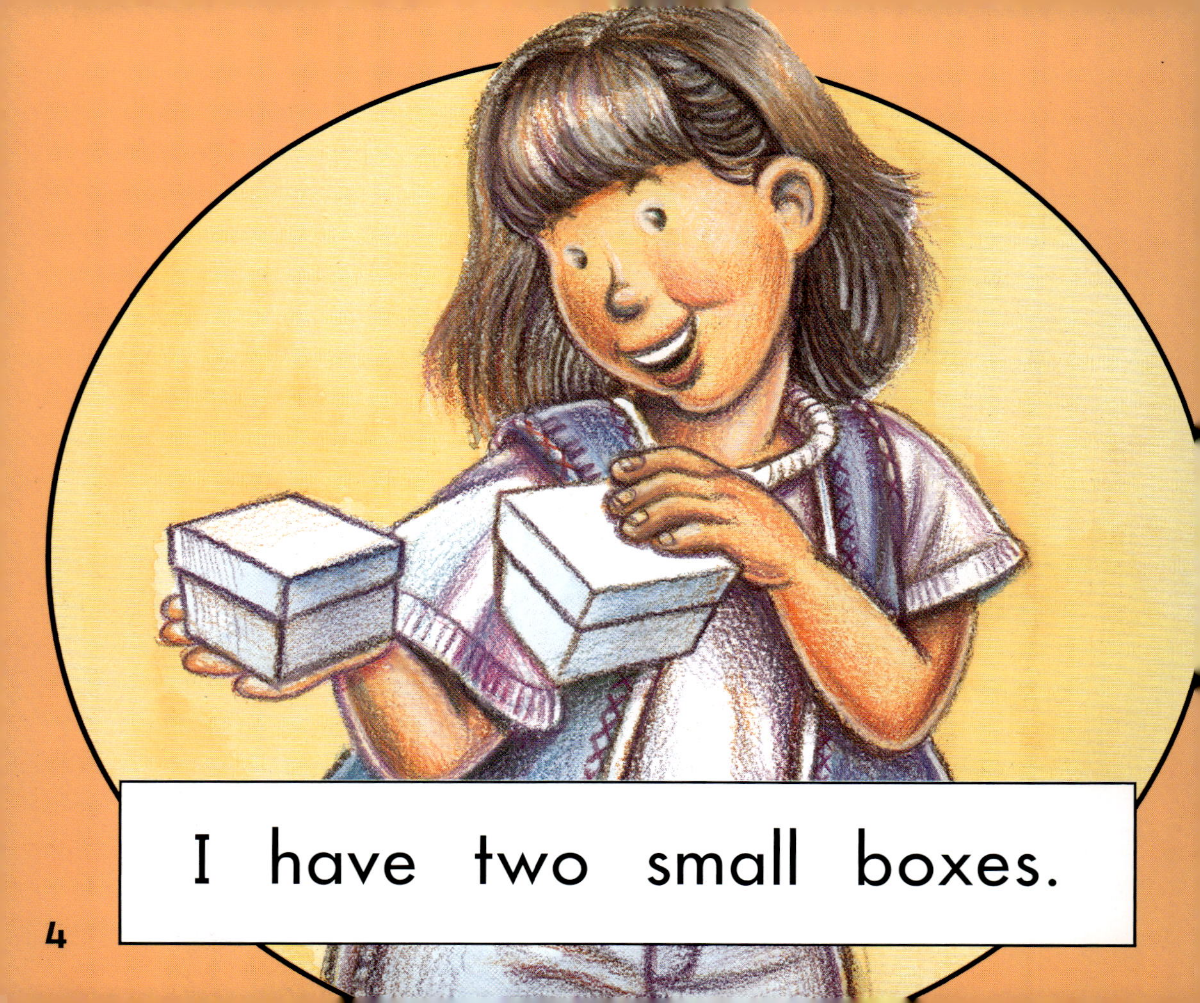

I have two small boxes.

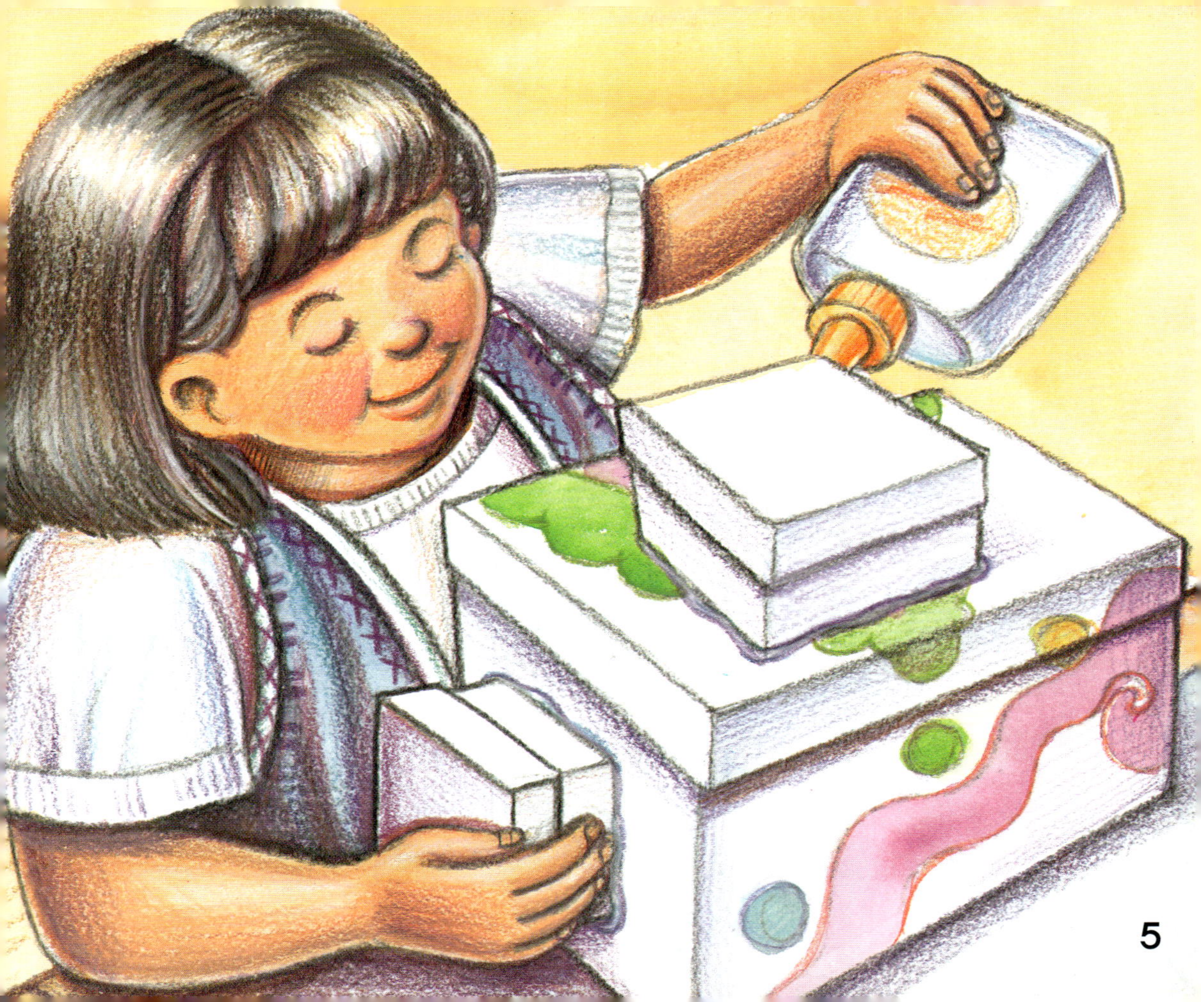

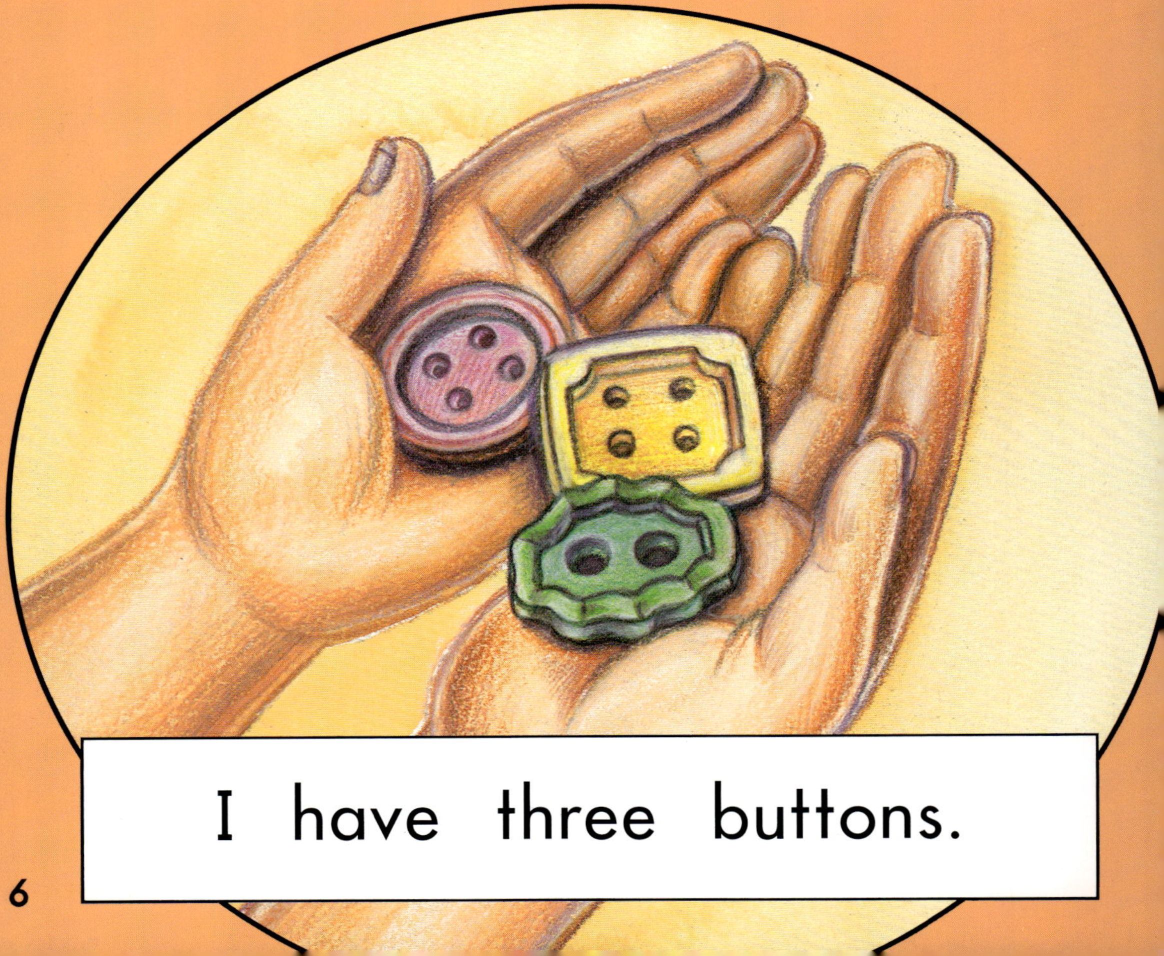

I have three buttons.

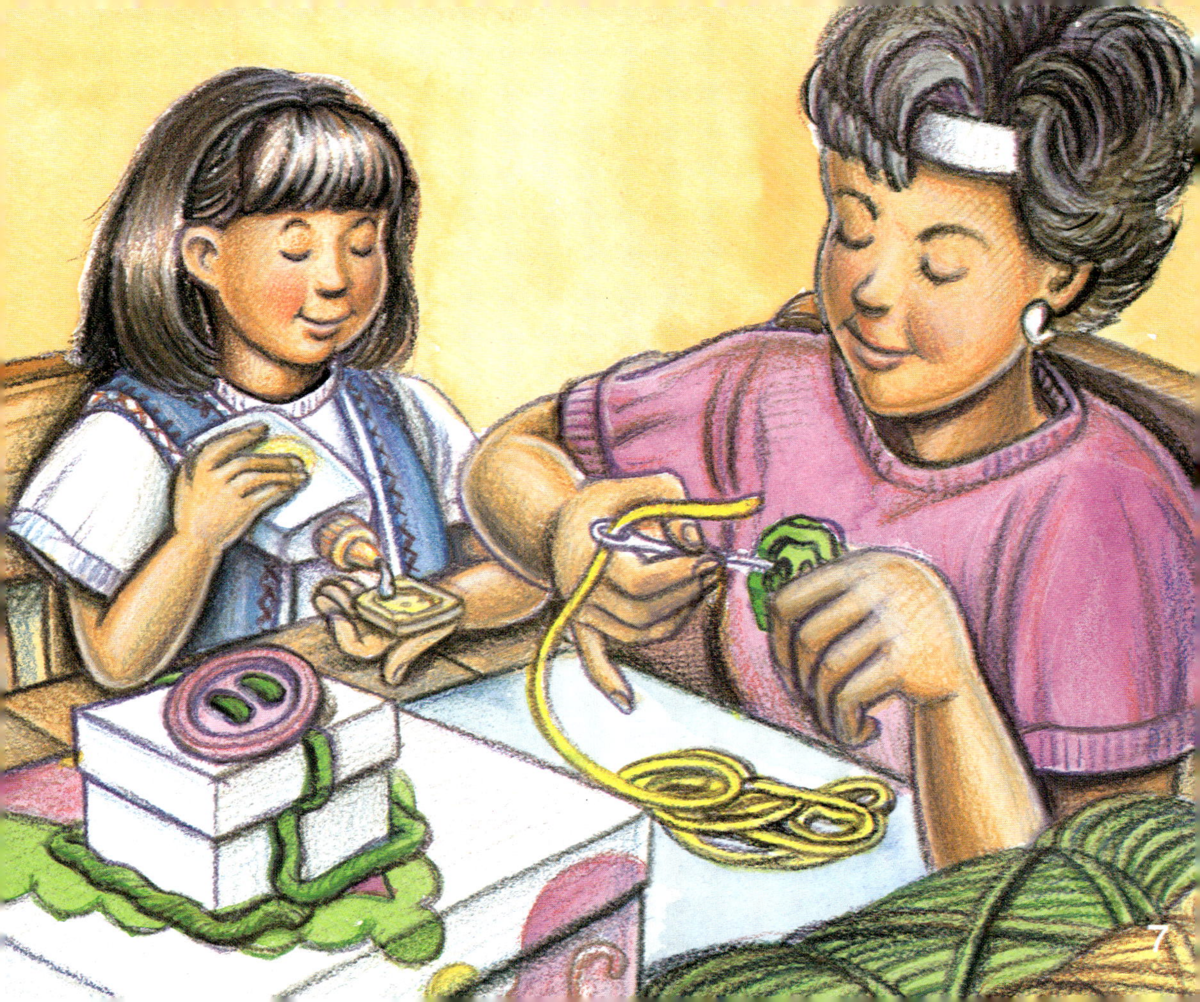

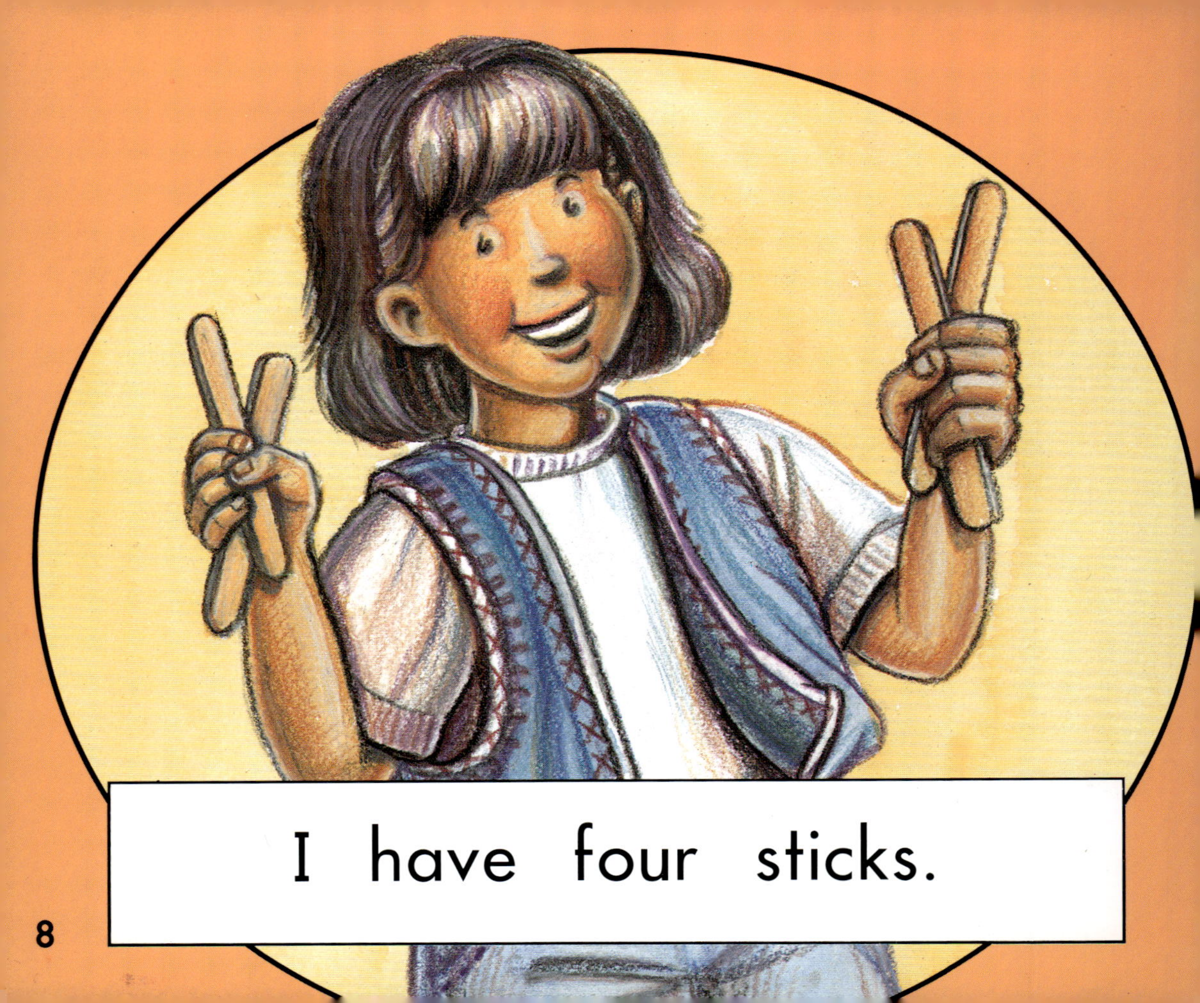

I have four sticks.

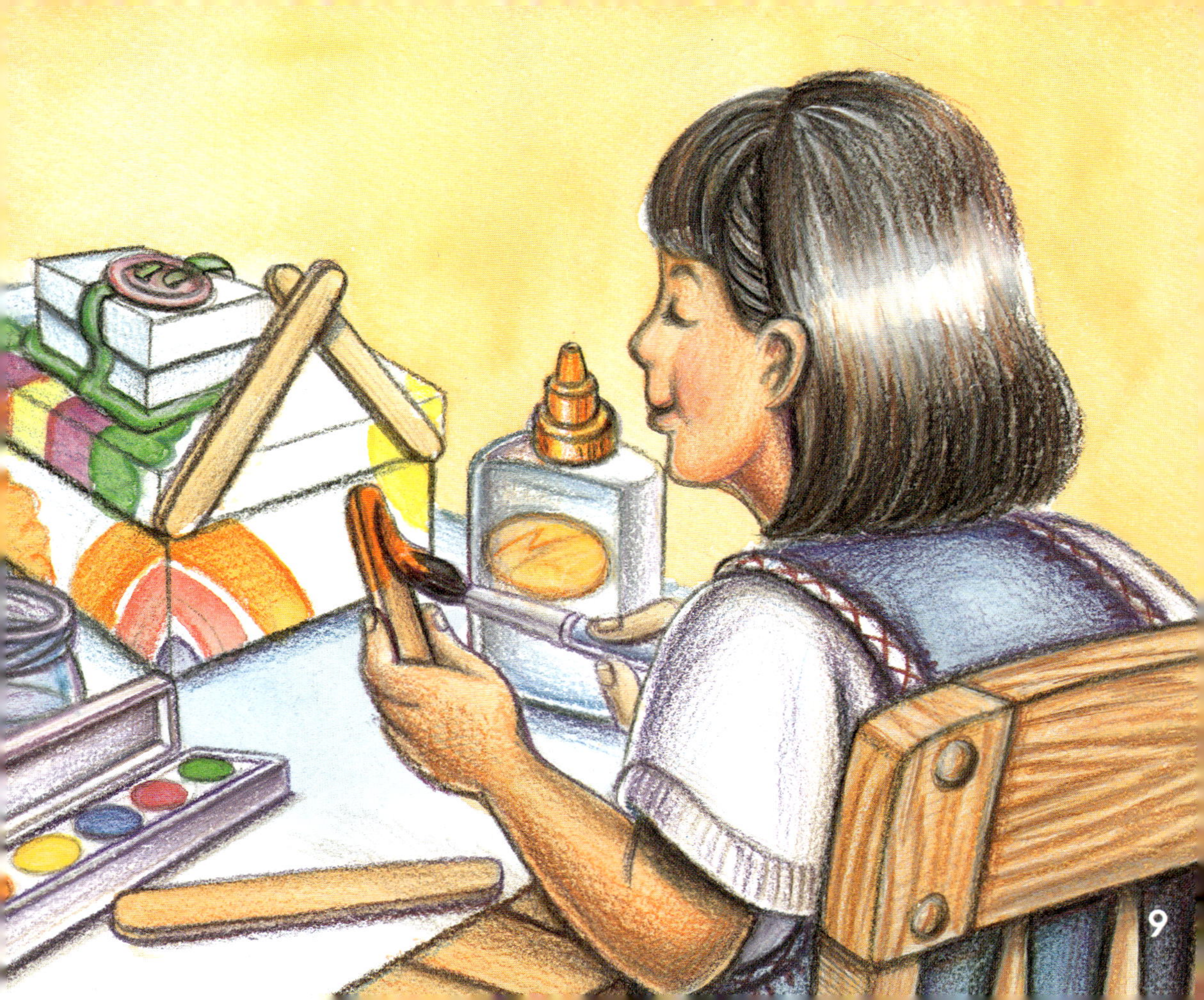

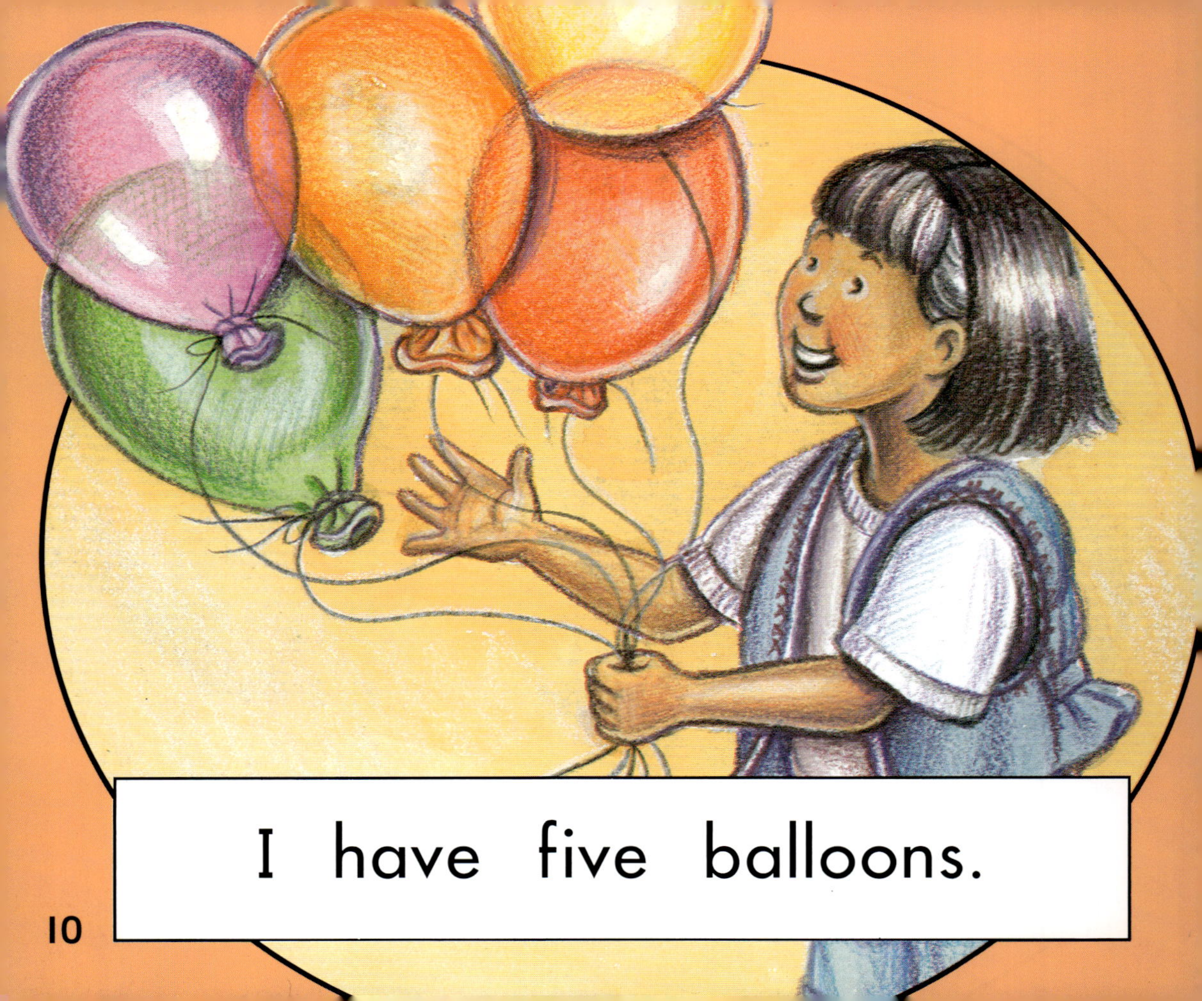

I have five balloons.

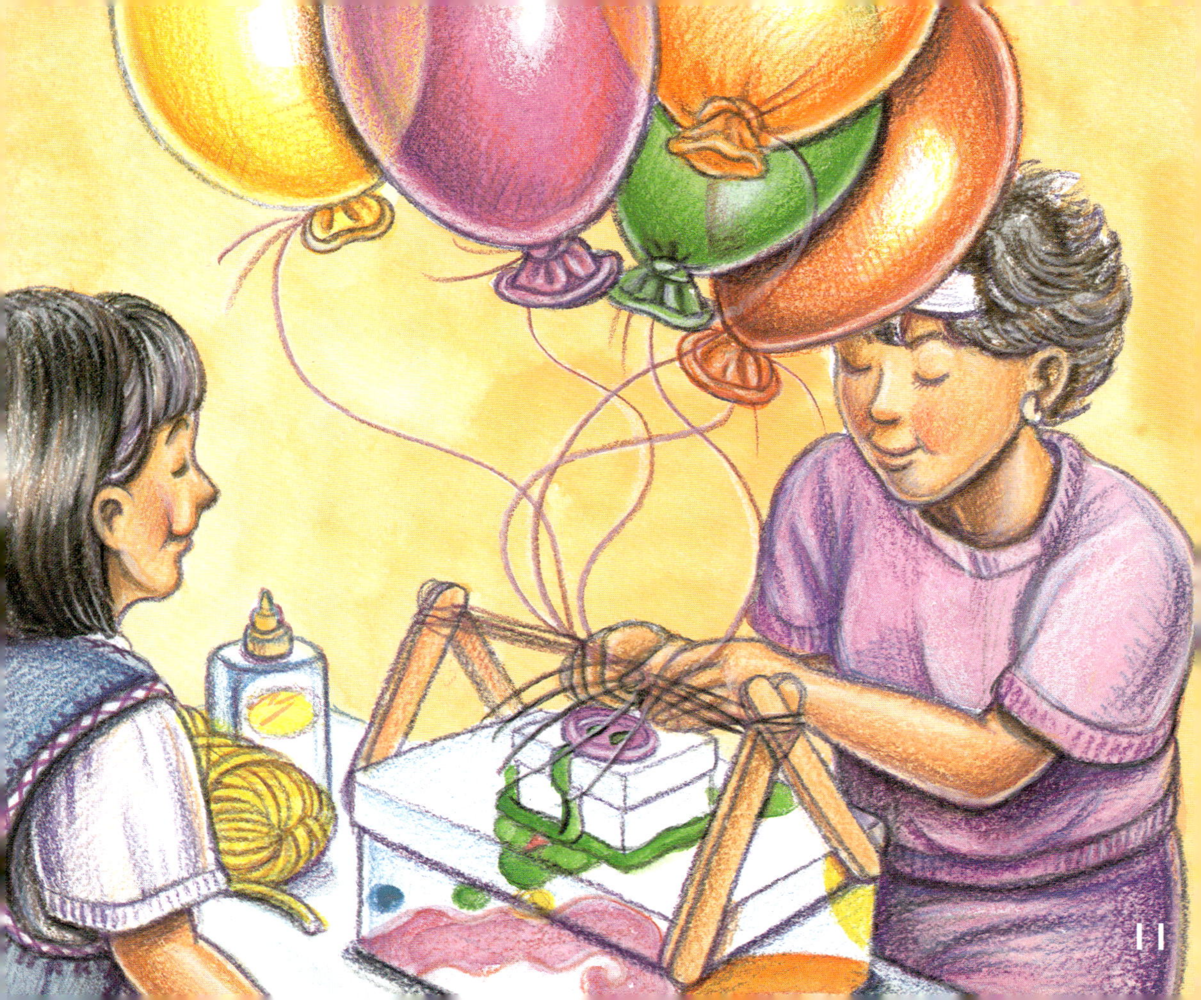

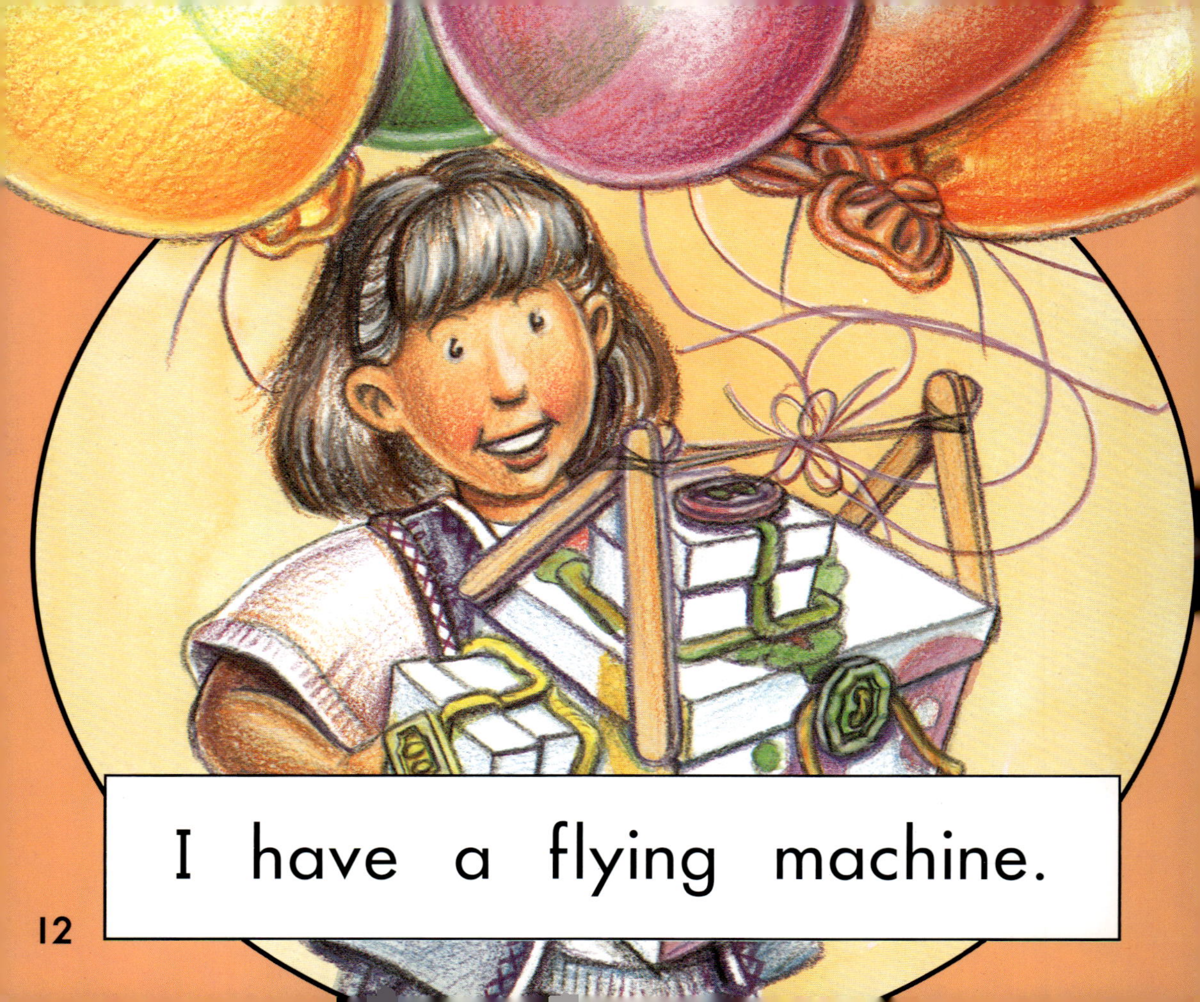

I have a flying machine.

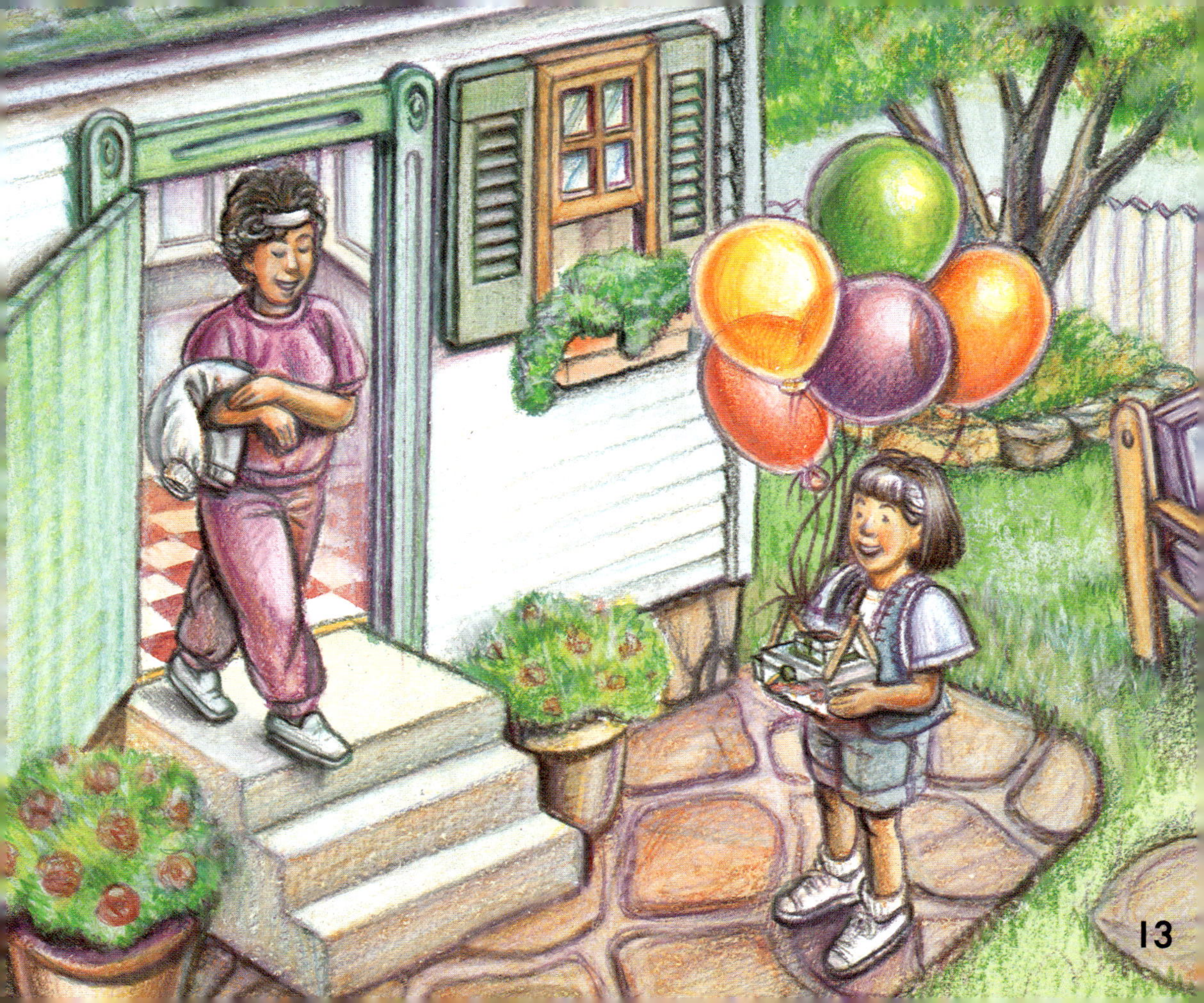

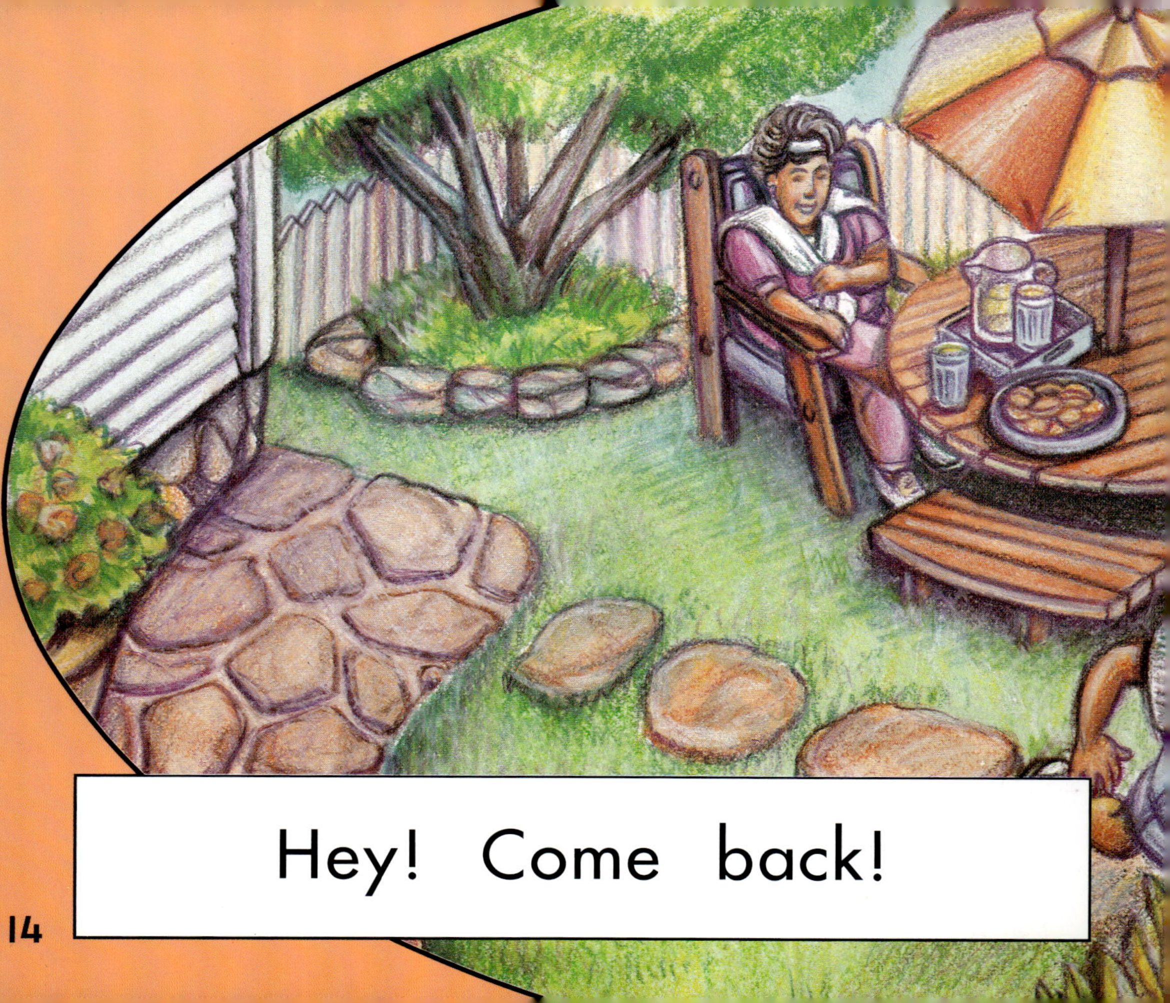

Hey! Come back!

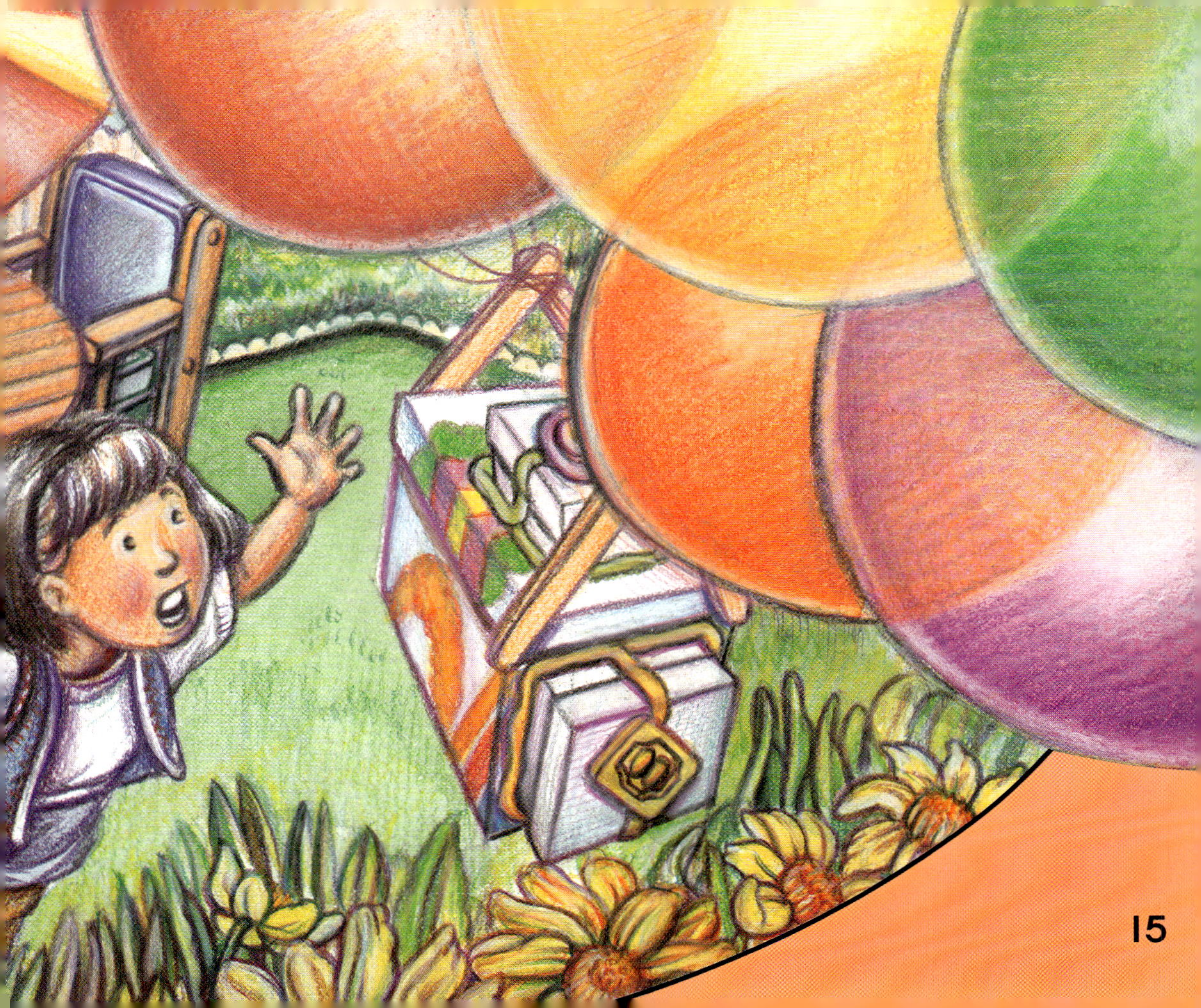

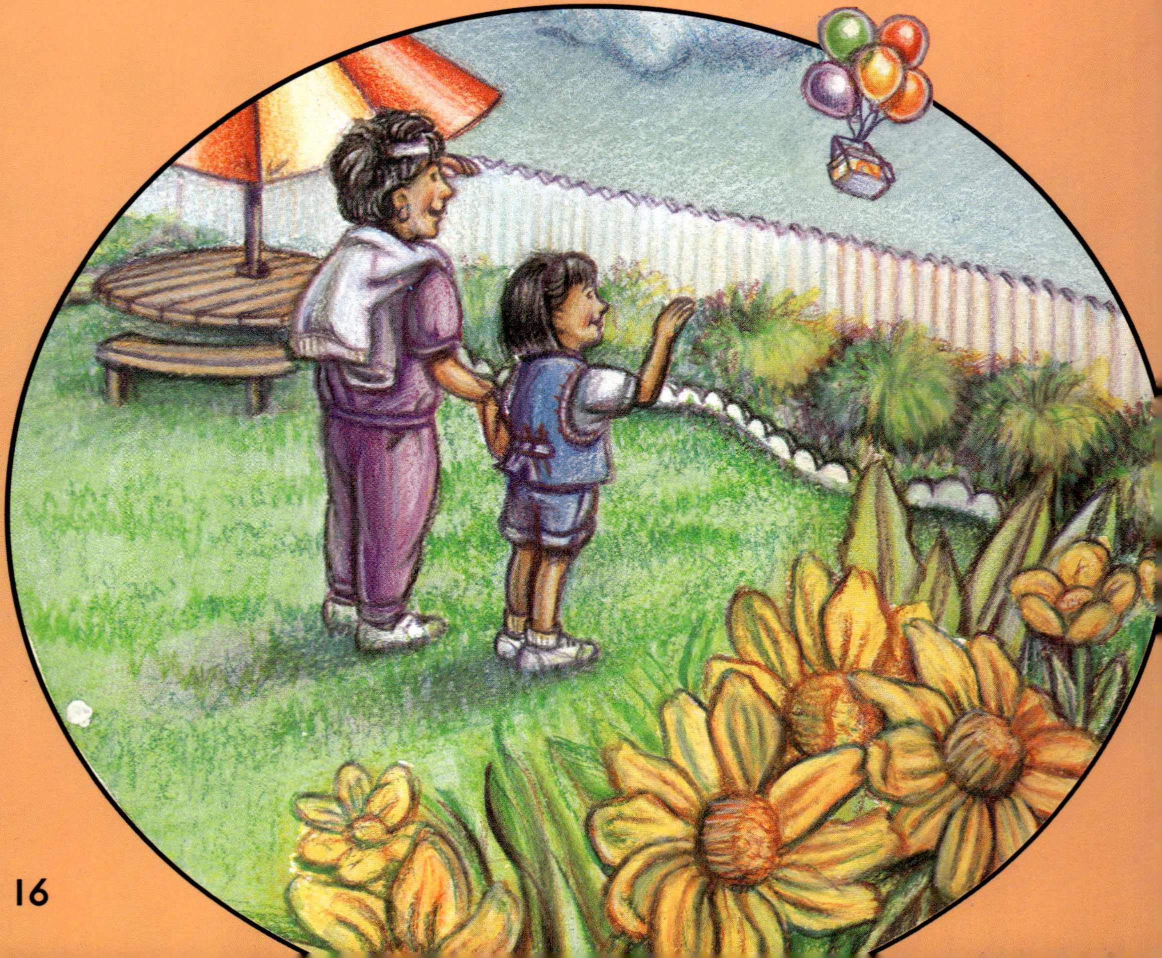